The Wacky Wedge

Julie Murray

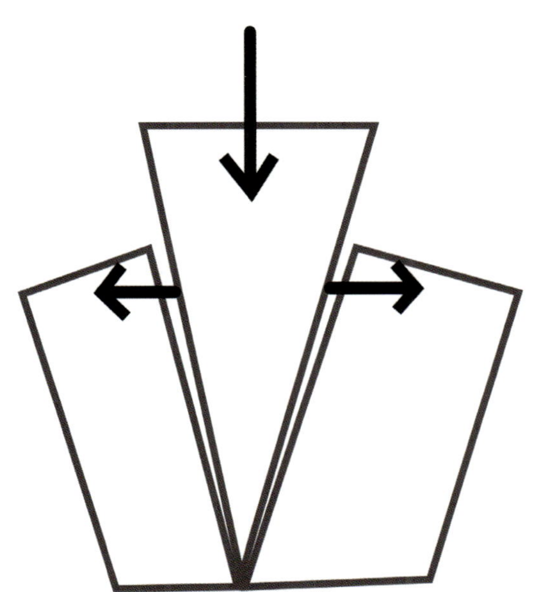

Abdo Kids Junior
is an Imprint of Abdo Kids
abdobooks.com

abdobooks.com

Published by Abdo Kids, a division of ABDO, P.O. Box 398166, Minneapolis, Minnesota 55439.

Printed in the United States of America, North Mankato, Minnesota.

052024

092024

Photo Credits: Getty Images, Shutterstock

Production Contributors: Teddy Borth, Jennie Forsberg, Grace Hansen

Design Contributors: Candice Keimig, Pakou Moua

Library of Congress Control Number: 2023948539

Publisher's Cataloging-in-Publication Data

Names: Murray, Julie, author.

Title: The wacky wedge / by Julie Murray

Description: Minneapolis, Minnesota : Abdo Kids, 2025 | Series: Simple machines | Includes online resources and index.

Identifiers: ISBN 9798384900634 (lib. bdg.) | ISBN 9798384901334 (ebook) | ISBN 9798384901686 (Read-to-me eBook)

Subjects: LCSH: Simple machines--Juvenile literature. | Wedges--Juvenile literature. | Chisels--Juvenile literature. | Machinery--Juvenile literature. | Hand tools--Juvenile literature.

Classification: DDC 621.8--dc23

Table of Contents

The Wacky Wedge

A wedge is a simple machine.

It is used to cut and divide things.

It is also used to hold things in place.

A wedge can be made up of one or two **inclined planes**.

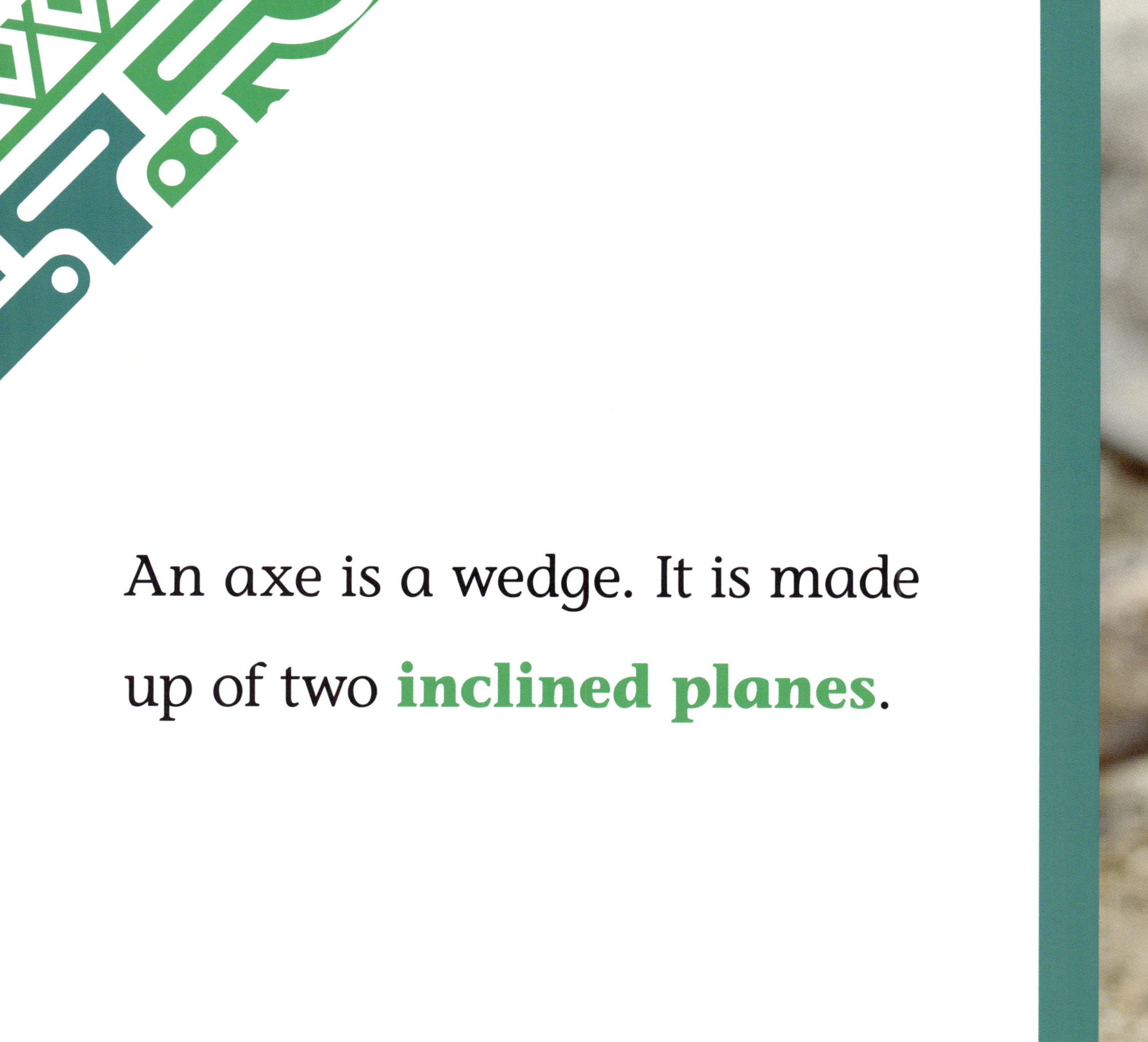

An axe is a wedge. It is made up of two **inclined planes**.

Force is needed to use a wedge.

force

Force is used to swing an axe.

This drives the axe into wood.

force

The wedge creates outward **force**. It splits the wood apart.

force

The wedge makes work easier!

Wedges Around You

ice scraper

peeler

spatula

zipper

Glossary

force
power, energy, or physical strength.

inclined plane
a sloping surface.

Index

Visit **abdokids.com** to access crafts, games, videos, and more!

Use Abdo Kids code

STK0634

or scan this QR code!